Machu Picchu

by Grace Hansen

abdopublishing.com

Published by Abdo Kids, a division of ABDO, P.O. Box 398166, Minneapolis, Minnesota 55439.

Printed in the United States of America, North Mankato, Minnesota.

102017

012018

THIS BOOK CONTAINS RECYCLED MATERIALS

Photo Credits: Granger Collection, iStock, North Wind Picture Archives, Shutterstock

Production Contributors: Teddy Borth, Jennie Forsberg, Grace Hansen

Design Contributors: Dorothy Toth, Laura Mitchell

Publisher's Cataloging in Publication Data

Names: Hansen, Grace, author.

Title: Machu Picchu / by Grace Hansen.

Description: Minneapolis, Minnesota : Abdo Kids, 2018. | Series: World wonders | Includes glossary, index and online resource (page 24).

Identifiers: LCCN 2017943220 | ISBN 9781532104428 (lib.bdg.) | ISBN 9781532105548 (ebook) | ISBN 9781532106101 (Read-to-me ebook)

Subjects: LCSH: Machu Picchu Site (Peru)--Juvenile literature. | Incas--History--Juvenile literature. | Inca architecture--Juvenile literature. | Peru--Antiquities--Juvenile literature.

Classification: DDC 985.37--dc23

LC record available at https://lccn.loc.gov/2017943220

Table of Contents

Machu Picchu

Machu Picchu is in Peru. It is
in the Andes Mountains.
It was built around 1450 CE.

Peru

The **Inca** people built Machu Picchu. It was a sacred place. It was also a place for Inca leaders.

Machu Picchu has more than 150 buildings. They are made from stone. The **Inca** did not use any **mortar**. They cut stones to fit perfectly together.

There is one very special structure. It was used as a solar clock. It told the **Inca** when it was **winter solstice**. This was the time to celebrate **Inti Raymi**.

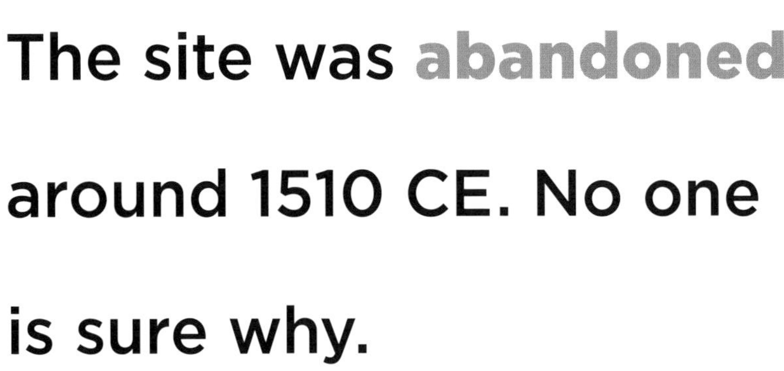

The site was **abandoned** around 1510 CE. No one is sure why.

The Spanish Invaders

Soon after, the Spanish came to South America. The Spanish destroyed many things. But they never found this sacred place. This was likely due to its **remote** location.

Rediscovering Machu Picchu

Few knew about Machu Picchu for more than 400 years. In 1911, Hiram Bingham visited the site. He was an explorer.

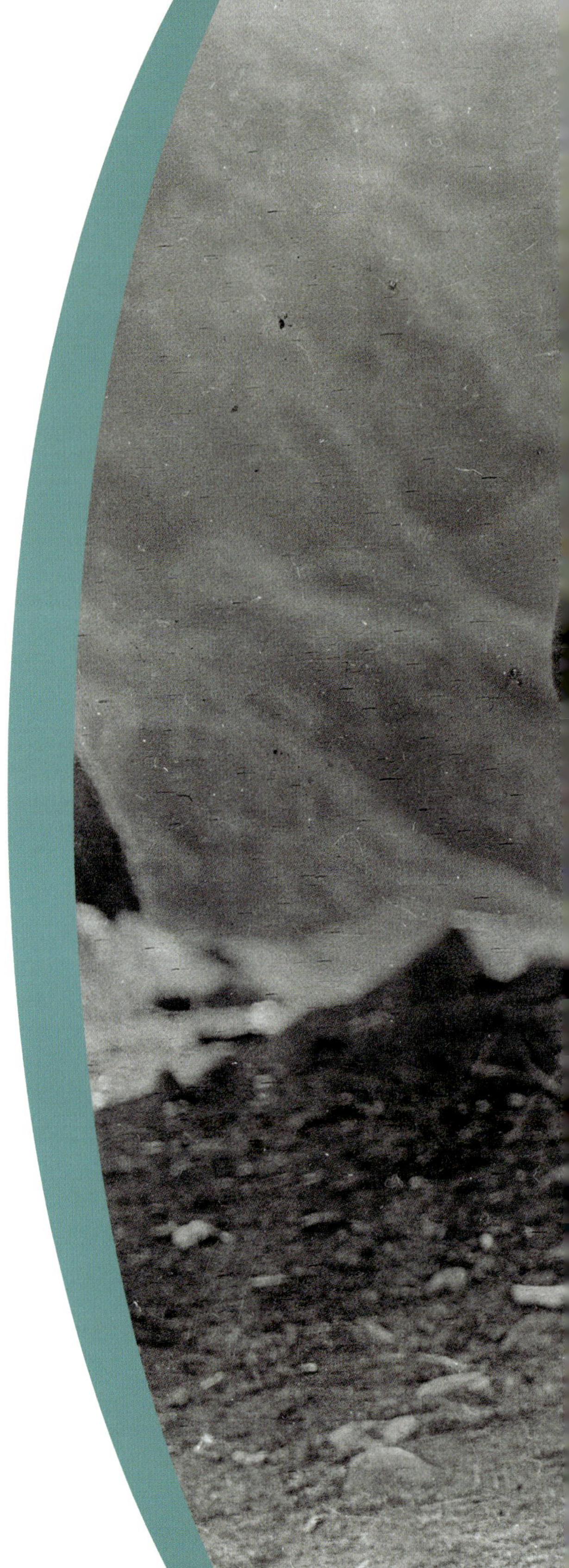

17

By then Machu Picchu was covered in jungle. But Bingham still knew how special it was. He made it known to the world.

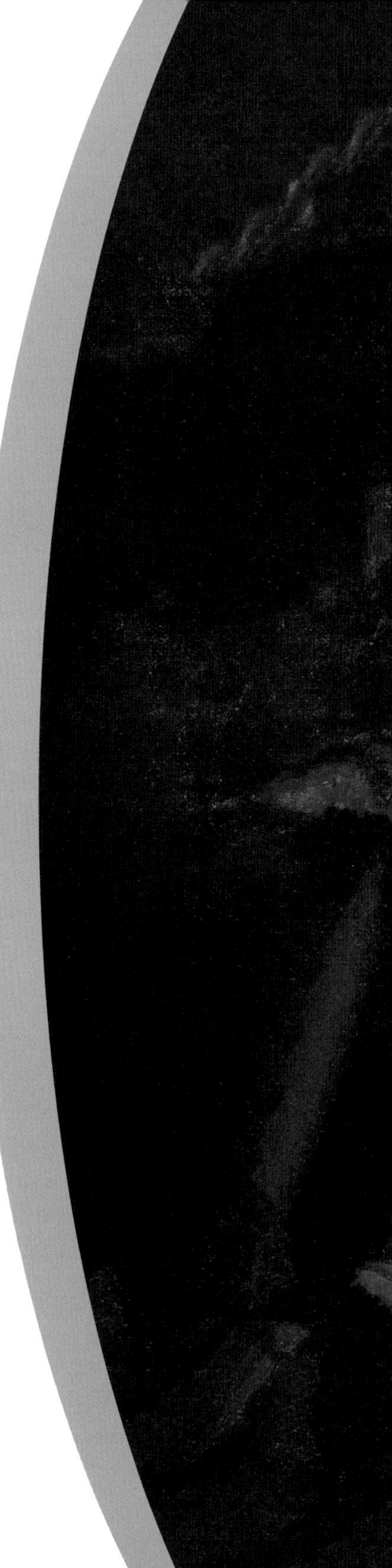

In 1983, Machu Picchu was protected by the United Nations. Many people visit each year.

More Facts

- Machu Picchu means "old peak" in the Quechua language.

- Other special structures that make up Machu Picchu include temples, houses, and sacred baths.

- The solar clock is called the Intihuatana Stone. The name means, "hitching post of the sun."

Glossary

abandon - to leave behind with no plan to return.

Inca - a member of any of the Quechuan peoples of Peru who had an empire until the Spanish conquest.

Inti Raymi - Quechua for "sun festival," a religious ceremony of the Incan empire to honor Inti, the Inca god of the sun.

mortar - a mixture that is used to hold bricks or stones in place.

remote - far from towns or human settlement.

winter solstice - June 21st is the shortest day of the year in the southern hemisphere, marking the start of winter.

Index

Visit **abdokids.com** and use this code to access crafts, games, videos, and more!